# On the Pathway with Paul

## Paul's Letter to the Philippians

LifeMark Publications

2500 Dallas Parkway, Suite 495

Plano, TX 75093

ISBN: 978-0-9890230-5-4

Design by Angeline Collier / Halo Creative
www.halocreative.com

# Table of Contents

# LIFEMARK
## M I N I S T R I E S

We all desire purpose in our life. What were we designed to do? What will fulfill us? What difference will our life make? The mission of LifeMark Ministries is to guide you to boldly use your God-given talents and abilities to make an eternal mark with your life – your **eMark.** We do this by equipping you through two avenues:

• **Learn** more about God and know Him more intimately.
• **Live** a life that reflects and honors Him.

To learn more about this ministry, visit our website:
**www.LifeMarkMinistries.org**

LifeMark Ministries was founded by Mark Schupbach, a businessman with a desire to use the experience, gifts, and talents he has been given by God to support and equip believers in their faith journey.

Mark's involvement with the church and ministry began more than 30 years ago. He has served as an elder and president on three church governing boards in both Wichita, Kansas, and Dallas, Texas. He was involved in Bible Study Fellowship for 17 years, including serving as the Men's Teaching Leader in Dallas for 9 years. In 2003, Mark founded Next Step Bible Study to encourage participants to seek a deeper, more intimate relationship with the Lord Jesus Christ. With a firm reliance on the Holy Spirit, Mark enjoys exhorting believers to get out of their "comfort zones" and fulfill their purpose.

Mark has been married to his wife, Marty, since 1969. They have 3 married daughters and 6 grandchildren.

George Reese is a retired attorney who has been blessed with the opportunity to devote a majority of his time to serious Bible study as well as helping others grow in their faith. He has had the privilege of assisting Mark with the preparation of the Next Step Bible Study curriculum since the study began in 2003.

In connection with his church, George teaches youth and young adult Sunday School classes as well as Bible survey courses (Genesis to Revelation). It has been especially rewarding for him to serve as a mentor to children in the process of being confirmed to Christ prior to joining the church. He has served on numerous church committees.

George and his wife, Pam, have been married for 31 years. They enjoy fishing for black bass at Lake Fork (Pam catches all the big ones), hiking in Jackson Hole, biking and Aggie football.

Each week you will complete the lesson preparation, meet with your small group to review your lesson, and then watch The Talk (live or on video). Start your lesson preparation with prayer, asking God to open your eyes to see the lessons He has for you. Before you begin the questions, we suggest you read through the assigned Bible verses 1-2 times in order to understand the context of the passage.

Each lesson is structured identically with the following sections:

**Questions** - Answer these in preparation for each week's study.

**Portrait of Paul** - Write down characteristics and attributes you see in Paul each week.

**Principles** - List lessons or principles you learn in the study.

**Path** - List the next steps you can take to walk the path God has for you. These should be practical, tangible steps that will encourage you to make progress but not overwhelm you.

**Prayer** - Write down your prayer for the week, asking God to help you apply what you've learned and strengthen you to take your "Next Steps."

**Precept** - Ponder this verse daily and allow it to penetrate your heart and mind.

**Notes from The Talk** - Take notes while you listen to "The Talk" by Mark Schupbach.

Keep in mind that this is a workbook, not a textbook. Don't be afraid to write in it, highlight it, circle key words – whatever it takes to help you absorb the content. We also recommend either purchasing a good Bible dictionary or using some online resources when you come across words or phrases with which you are not familiar. Here are a few web sites we recommend:

**www.Bible.org**

**www.BlueLetterBible.org**

**www.GotQuestions.org**

Before we get started, take a minute to write down what you hope to gain from this study:

_____

_____

_____

_____

_____

Like anything, the more time and effort you invest in this study, the more you will grow in your walk with God. Most importantly, pray for God to guide you and for the Holy Spirit to reveal God's truth to you as you study and seek to apply His Word.

# *Acknowledgements*

Dear Friend,

Paul was a fascinating man. How did a man who is arguably one of the worst persecutors of the church in the history of mankind become it's greatest proponent?

**He encountered Jesus.**

That moment of transformation on the road to Damascus was so powerful that Paul's purpose in life changed from persecuting believers to preaching the gospel of Jesus Christ.

If you're reading this study, you likely aren't overtly fighting against Christianity like Paul was when he encountered God. However, we all battle against the temptations of sin that affect our fellowship with the Lord. We need others to come alongside and battle with us – to share in this journey of discipleship, just as Paul did.

Paul's letters to the churches, many of which he founded and fostered, contain words of thanksgiving, encouragement, exhortation, and warning. These words are just as applicable today as they were then.

It is my prayer that through this study, our *"love may abound more and more in knowledge and depth of insight"* so that we may be able to *"discern what is best and may be pure and blameless for the day of Christ, filled with the fruit of righteousness that comes through Jesus Christ – to the glory and praise of God"* (Philippians 1:9, NIV).

The development of this study has been a labor of love, and I'd like to express my gratitude specifically to George and Pam Reese, Jennifer Hicks, Kathy Prather, and Angeline Collier for using their gifts to help us all draw closer to our Father.

For His glory,

# Lesson 1: *Joy in Chains*

## Read Philippians 1:1-11

1.  To whom was the letter addressed?

    _____

    _____

    _____

    _____

    _____

2.  What was Paul's situation?  (1:13; Acts 28:16, 30)

    _____

    _____

    _____

    _____

    _____

3.  What were the reasons for Paul's joy and affection for the believers at Philippi? (vv. 3-8)

    _____

    _____

    _____

    _____

    _____

4.  What is the difference between how Paul used the word *joy* and the way the word is used in our culture?

    _____

    _____

    _____

    _____

    _____

5.  How can you experience continuing joy regardless of your circumstances? How can you suppress it?  (Galatians 5:22)

    _____

    _____

    _____

    _____

    _____

6.  Explain what Paul meant by what he said in verse 6 and how you can apply it.

    _____

    _____

    _____

    _____

    _____

7.  Where do you see evidence in your life that God is continuing a good work in you?

    _____

    _____

    _____

    _____

    _____

8.   Explain what Paul wanted for the Philippians in verses 9-11.

_____

_____

_____

_____

_____

9.   What is the difference between spiritual fruit and religious activity?  (v. 11; John 15:1-5; Galatians 5:22-23; Ephesians 2:10)

_____

_____

_____

_____

_____

## Read Philippians 1:12-26

10.   How did Paul's imprisonment serve to advance the gospel rather than hinder it?

_____

_____

_____

_____

_____

11.   What distinguished the two types of evangelists described in verses 15-17?

_____

_____

_____

_____

_____

12. What was the reason for Paul's rejoicing in verse 18, and what do you learn from this about Paul?

_____

_____

_____

_____

13. What was the reason for Paul's rejoicing in verse 19, and what do you learn about Paul's faith?

_____

_____

_____

_____

14. Explain what Paul hoped for in verse 20 in light of his uncertain future. What do you learn from this?

_____

_____

_____

_____

_____

15. What alternatives did Paul see for himself in verses 21-26?  (2 Corinthians 5:1-9)

_____

_____

_____

_____

16. What alternative did Paul think was best?  Why?

_____

_____

_____

_____

# *Pause with Paul*

## Portrait of Paul
What attributes and characteristics of Paul did you see in this week's lesson?

_____

_____

_____

_____

## Principles
What principles did you learn in this lesson?

_____

_____

_____

## Path
What tangible steps can you take to apply what you've learned this week?

_____

_____

_____

## Prayer
As you think about what you have learned in this lesson, write down a prayer asking God to strengthen you to take your "Next Steps," draw closer to Him, and become more Christ-like in your attitude and actions.

_____

_____

_____

## Precept
Ponder this verse daily and allow it to penetrate your heart and mind. Ask God to help you apply it in your life.

*He who began a good work in you will carry it on to completion until the day of Christ.* - **Philippians 1:6b (NIV)**

# Notes from the Talk

# Lesson 2: *Having the Mind of Christ*

## Read Philippians 1:27-30

1. How were the Philippians to respond to trials and suffering? (vv. 27-28)

   _____

   _____

   _____

   _____

   _____

2. What did Paul mean by what he said in verse 28b?

   _____

   _____

   _____

   _____

   _____

3. What do you learn about suffering for the sake of Christ from verses 29-30 and how will you apply it? (Matthew 5:10; Romans 8:16-17; 1 Peter 4:12-14)

   _____

   _____

   _____

   _____

   _____

4.  What steps can you take in order to maintain an attitude of joy while experiencing trials and suffering?  (Romans 5:1-5; James 1:2-5)

_____

_____

_____

_____

_____

**Read Philippians 2:1-5**

5.  What does it mean to be united with Christ?  (Romans 6:3-11)

_____

_____

_____

_____

_____

6.  How should being united with Christ and fellow believers promote spiritual unity in the church?  (vv. 1-2; John 17:20-24)

_____

_____

_____

_____

_____

7.  Define humility according to Paul and how it can be expressed.  (vv. 3-5)

_____

_____

_____

_____

_____

8. How does humility affect your spiritual growth?  Why?

_____

_____

_____

_____

_____

9. What is pride?  In what areas of your life do you struggle with pride?

_____

_____

_____

_____

10. What are indications that you are being prideful in your relationship with God?

_____

_____

_____

_____

11. What are indications that you are being prideful in your relationships with others?

_____

_____

_____

_____

12. What practical steps can you take to maintain humility in your relationships with God and others?

_____

_____

_____

_____

13. Explain what Paul meant in his description of Christ in verses 6a and 8a. What did he *not* mean?

_____

_____

_____

_____

_____

14. Using verses 6-8, explain how Christ expressed His humility in attitude and action.

_____

_____

_____

_____

_____

15. How you can have the same attitude or mindset as Jesus in your relationships with God and others? (Mark 10:43b-45; John 13:14-17)

_____

_____

_____

_____

_____

16. Using verses 9-11, describe God's exaltation of Jesus and the extent of Christ's power.

_____

_____

_____

_____

_____

# Pause with Paul

## Portrait of Paul
What attributes and characteristics of Paul did you see in this week's lesson?

_____

_____

_____

_____

## Principles
What principles did you learn in this lesson?

_____

_____

_____

## Path
What tangible steps can you take to apply what you've learned this week?

_____

_____

_____

## Prayer
As you think about what you have learned in this lesson, write down a prayer asking God to strengthen you to take your "Next Steps," draw closer to Him, and become more Christ-like in your attitude and actions.

_____

_____

_____

## Precept
Ponder this verse daily and allow it to penetrate your heart and mind.  Ask God to help you apply it in your life.

_In your relationships with one another, have the same mindset as Christ Jesus._  **- Philippians 2:5 (NIV)**

# Notes from the Talk

# Lesson 3: *The Heart of a Servant*

Read Philippians 2:12-18

1. What is God's ultimate goal for a believer during his or her lifetime? (Romans 8:28-29)

   _____

   _____

   _____

   _____

   _____

   _____

2. Explain what Paul said in verses 12-13 regarding a believer's spiritual growth and development (sanctification) in pursuit of that goal.

   _____

   _____

   _____

   _____

   _____

   _____

3. What is God's role and a believer's role in this process? (John 15:1-5; Romans 12:1-2)

   _____

   _____

   _____

   _____

   _____

4.  What did Paul want the Philippians to be and do in order to work out God's purposes and plans in their daily lives?  (vv. 14-16)

_____

_____

_____

_____

_____

5.  How does habitual complaining affect your Christian example and the lives of those around you?

_____

_____

_____

_____

_____

6.  How can a negative attitude affect your spiritual growth?  How can you combat that negativity?

_____

_____

_____

_____

_____

7.  What did Paul mean by what he said in verses 17-18?  What do you learn about Paul?

_____

_____

_____

_____

_____

8.  Do you continue to show a genuine interest in people you introduced to the gospel or helped spiritually in the past?  Why is this important?

_____

_____

_____

_____

_____

9.  What do you learn about Paul's relationship with Timothy?  (1 Timothy 1:2)

_____

_____

_____

_____

_____

10.  When and why was Paul sending Timothy to Philippi?

_____

_____

_____

_____

_____

11.  What qualities of Timothy made him valuable to Paul and to the church at Philippi?

_____

_____

_____

_____

_____

12. What do you learn from what Paul said in verses 20-21 and how should you apply it? (Matthew 25:37-40)

_____

_____

_____

_____

Read Philippians 2:25-30

13. What was Epaphroditus' role and how had he assisted Paul? (Philippians 4:18)

_____

_____

_____

_____

14. Why was Paul sending Epaphroditus back to Philippi?

_____

_____

_____

_____

15. How had Epaphroditus demonstrated a Christ-like attitude and behavior?

_____

_____

_____

_____

16. Why should you honor someone you know like Epaphroditus and how will you do it? (v. 29)

_____

_____

_____

_____

# Pause with Paul

## Portrait of Paul
What attributes and characteristics of Paul did you see in this week's lesson?

_____

_____

_____

_____

## Principles
What principles did you learn in this lesson?

_____

_____

_____

## Path
What tangible steps can you take to apply what you've learned this week?

_____

_____

_____

## Prayer
As you think about what you have learned in this lesson, write down a prayer asking God to strengthen you to take your "Next Steps," draw closer to Him, and become more Christ-like in your attitude and actions.

_____

_____

_____

## Precept
Ponder this verse daily and allow it to penetrate your heart and mind. Ask God to help you apply it in your life.

*Do everything without grumbling or arguing, so that you may become blameless and pure children of God without fault in a warped and crooked generation.* - **Philippians 2:14-15a (NIV)**

# Notes from the Talk

# Lesson 4: *Righteousness Through Faith in Jesus Christ*

**Read Philippians 3:1-10**

1. What was the source of the controversy between the Jewish legalists and Paul? (v. 2; Acts 15:1-5)

   _____

   _____

   _____

   _____

   _____

2. How did Paul describe true believers in verse 3? What did he mean by *the flesh*? (Deuteronomy 30:6)

   _____

   _____

   _____

   _____

   _____

3. Why did Paul choose to boast about his impressive credentials and his past confidence in the flesh in verses 4-6?

   _____

   _____

   _____

   _____

   _____

4. What should you tell people who place their trust in themselves, their ancestry, their religious activities or their achievements?

_____

_____

_____

_____

_____

5. What did Paul conclude about the true value of his ancestry, religion and achievements in verses 7-9?  What do you learn from it?

_____

_____

_____

_____

_____

_____

6. Explain what it means to *know* Christ and why this is important.  (v. 8; Luke 13:22-27; John 17:3)

_____

_____

_____

_____

_____

_____

7. Are you willing to give up all things for the sake of knowing Christ Jesus, your Lord? Why or why not?

_____

_____

_____

_____

_____

_____

8. Explain the difference between a righteousness of one's own that comes from good works or obedience to the law and the righteousness that comes by God's grace through faith. (v. 9; Romans 3:19-26; Ephesians 2:8-9)

_____

_____

_____

_____

_____

9. Explain the three ways Paul wanted a deeper intimacy with and knowledge of Christ by sharing in His experiences. (vv. 10-11)

_____

_____

_____

_____

_____

## Read Philippians 3:12-16

10. What was Paul saying about his sanctification and need for continuous spiritual growth? What was Paul's goal?

_____

_____

_____

_____

_____

11. What do you learn from verses 13b-14 and 16, and how will you apply it?

_____

_____

_____

_____

12. What from your past is hindering your spiritual growth?  What steps can you take to free yourself from your past and press on?

_____

_____

_____

_____

Read Philippians 3:17-21

13. Why did the Philippians need examples like Paul to follow?

_____

_____

_____

14. Explain Paul's description of the legalists and false teachers in verses 18-19.  Who are they today?

_____

_____

_____

15. How did Paul describe believers and their heavenly hope?  (vv. 20-21; 1 Corinthians 15:49-53; 1 Thessalonians 4:13-17)

_____

_____

_____

_____

16. How does focusing on your citizenship in heaven change the way you live today? (2 Corinthians 4:16-18; 5:6-10)

_____

_____

_____

_____

# Pause with Paul

## Portrait of Paul
What attributes and characteristics of Paul did you see in this week's lesson?

_____

_____

_____

_____

## Principles
What principles did you learn in this lesson?

_____

_____

_____

## Path
What tangible steps can you take to apply what you've learned this week?

_____

_____

_____

## Prayer
As you think about what you have learned in this lesson, write down a prayer asking God to strengthen you to take your "Next Steps," draw closer to Him, and become more Christ-like in your attitude and actions.

_____

_____

_____

## Precept
Ponder this verse daily and allow it to penetrate your heart and mind. Ask God to help you apply it in your life.

*I consider everything a loss because of the surpassing worth of knowing Christ Jesus my Lord, for whose sake I have lost all things.* - Philippians 3:8a (NIV)

# Notes from the Talk

# Lesson 5: *Focus on Joy and Contentment*

Read Philippians 4:1-9

1.  What seemed to be interrupting the peace and unity in the church, and what was Paul's solution?

    _____

    _____

    _____

    _____

2.  How does rejoicing in the Lord change your attitude about your problems?

    _____

    _____

    _____

    _____

3.  Why do you think Paul linked rejoicing and gentleness in verses 4-5?

    _____

    _____

    _____

    _____

4.  How did Paul tell the church to handle worry and anxiety in verses 6-7?

    _____

    _____

    _____

    _____

5.  How is the peace that God offers different from worldly peace?
    (John 14:27; Galatians 5:22)

    _____

    _____

    _____

    _____

    _____

6.  What does persistent worry and anxiety over problems say about you?
    (Matthew 6:25-34)

    _____

    _____

    _____

    _____

    _____

    _____

7.  Give some examples of what Paul was talking about in verse 8.

    _____

    _____

    _____

    _____

    _____

8.  Why is guarding your heart and mind so important but so difficult?  (James 1:14-15)

    _____

    _____

    _____

    _____

    _____

9. What steps can you take daily to focus on thoughts that are excellent and praiseworthy? How will this lead to peace with God and peace within?

_____
_____
_____
_____
_____

10. What is Paul's main point in verse 9? How will you apply it and what will be the result? (Philippians 3:17)

_____
_____
_____
_____
_____

## Read Philippians 4:10-20

11. What was Paul's secret to inner contentment under any circumstances and how can you apply it to your life?

_____
_____
_____
_____
_____

12. How have you learned to be content with what God has given you even though it may be less than what you desire?

_____
_____
_____
_____

13. Why is it as difficult to be content with plenty as it is to be content with need?
    (1 Timothy 6:6-10)

    _____

    _____

    _____

    _____

    _____

14. Why was Paul especially grateful for the support of the Philippians?  (vv. 14-16)

    _____

    _____

    _____

    _____

    _____

15. What did Paul mean by what he said in verses 17-19, and what do you learn from it?

    _____

    _____

    _____

    _____

    _____

    _____

16. What are three things you have learned from Paul during the course of this study?
    How have you put them into practice and what have been the results?

    _____

    _____

    _____

    _____

    _____

    _____

# Pause with Paul

## Portrait of Paul
What attributes and characteristics of Paul did you see in this week's lesson?

_____

_____

_____

## Principles
What principles did you learn in this lesson?

_____

_____

_____

## Path
What tangible steps can you take to apply what you've learned this week?

_____

_____

_____

## Prayer
As you think about what you have learned in this lesson, write down a prayer asking God to strengthen you to take your "Next Steps," draw closer to Him, and become more Christ-like in your attitude and actions.

_____

_____

_____

## Precept
Ponder this verse daily and allow it to penetrate your heart and mind. Ask God to help you apply it in your life.

*Finally, brothers and sisters, whatever is true, whatever is noble, whatever is right, whatever is pure, whatever is lovely, whatever is admirable – if anything is excellent or praiseworthy – think about such things.*
**- Philippians 4:8 (NIV)**

# Notes from the Talk

1.  How did this study help you know and love God more in a deeper personal relationship and fellowship?

    _____

    _____

    _____

    _____

    _____

    _____

    _____

2.  In what ways are you more obedient to Jesus and a closer imitation of Him?

    _____

    _____

    _____

    _____

    _____

    _____

    _____

3.  What part of this study did you enjoy the most and why?

    _____

    _____

    _____

    _____

    _____

    _____

    _____

# Congratulations!

You have completed this study of Philippians – great job! We pray that you have been challenged by Paul's teachings and his personal example and that you have applied what you have learned this year to grow closer to our Lord.

It's important that you don't stop now! Here are some suggestions to help you continue to grow:

**Daily Prayer:** Get in the habit of starting each day with prayer. It's a conversation between you and God. Talk with Him about your day. Praise Him and share your concerns. Ask Him to fill you with His Spirit and guide your decisions each day. Strive to keep Him at the forefront of your thoughts.

**Daily Bible Reading:** Since you have been studying Paul's letters, perhaps it would be good to spend some time reading through the gospels to learn more about Jesus, the man whose life, death, and resurrection inspired Paul's transformation. We would also recommend reading Psalms and Proverbs which are wonderful books full of practical wisdom to apply in your life.

**Start Another Study:** We have a variety of studies available, including some of Paul's other writings as well as an in-depth study on the life of Jesus called Mosaic of the Master (volumes I and II). There are also a number of excellent Bible studies available at your local Christian bookstore or online. Regardless of which one you select, the important thing is to continue to study His Word!

**Visit our Website:** There you will find additional studies, tips, encouragement, and resources to help you in your walk with God. Visit our blog for devotionals and announcements, and follow us on Facebook and Twitter for daily encouragement.

We would love to hear from you! Please send your thoughts and feedback on this study to us by emailing: **info@lifemarkministries.org**. Share how this study has impacted your life and what you have learned through it.

www.LifeMarkMinistries.org
www.Facebook.com/LifeMarkMinistries
www.Twitter.com/LifeMarkMin

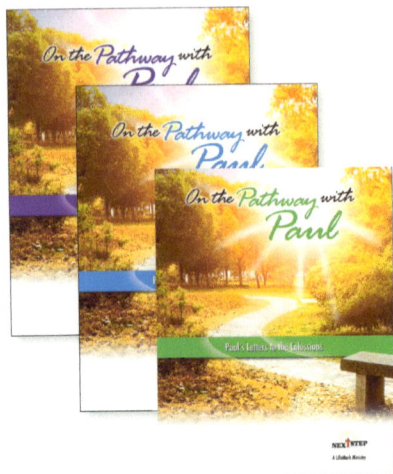

## On the Pathway with Paul

For centuries, letters have been used to communicate news, pertinent information, and personal stories. Sometimes they express love and joy, and other times they convey desperation and grief. Before the days of telephones and technology, letters were often the only way to converse with family and friends. When received, they were treasured as long-awaited gifts.

So it was with letters authored by the Apostle Paul. His letters to the churches flowed from his heart as he both praised their faithfulness and exhorted them to live lives worthy of the gospel of Jesus Christ.

Our new series, *On the Pathway With Paul*, will help you apply Paul's teachings to your life and be transformed by the study of God's Word.

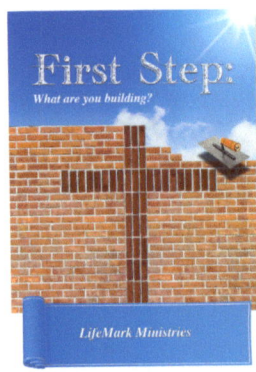

## First Step: Laying the Foundation for a God-honoring Life

In any building project, the most critical stage is laying a solid foundation. It is the same for our Christianity, too. If we know the basics of our faith, then we will be able to weather the storms of life.

This 10-week study is designed to ground you in those basics. Whether you are a new believer or someone who has been a Christian for years but wants to review the foundations of your faith, you will find this study to be helpful. The following five topics are covered, with two weeks on each topic: God the Father, The Bible, God the Son, God the Holy Spirit, and The Holy Trinity. For each topic, there will be verses to read, questions to answer, and a summary of the video. The videos are available separately as part of the First Step Leader's Kit.

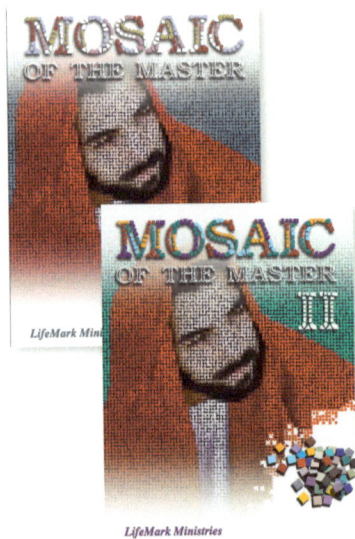

## Mosaic of the Master

Jesus was born. He served. He died and was resurrected.

We all know the basics of the greatest story in history. Most of us have heard the details for years. We celebrate at Christmas and Easter every year, and we often quote famous passages from the Bible.

However, those basics are simply vital pieces in the mosaic of Who Jesus is. The four Gospel authors give a much more in-depth and thorough picture of Jesus — His teachings, His miracles, His submission to the Father, His love and compassion for the least among us, His very heart.

Each piece will show you a different aspect of Jesus through the eyes of Matthew, Mark, Luke, and John. You will be challenged to grow in new ways as you piece together Jesus' story and see the beautiful mosaic God painted of His Son through His Word. ***It will change your own life story!***

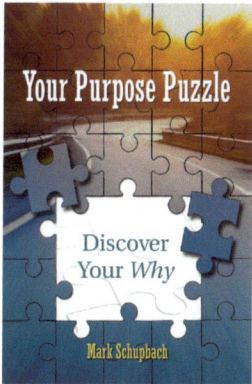

### Your Purpose Puzzle: Discover Your *Why*

Ponder your life for a moment.

Why are you living in your town? Why do you have the job you have? Why are you in a specific relationship? Why are you living in your current conditions, whatever they might be? God has a purpose for everyone — a purpose that He determined for us before we were even born. He created us specifically for this purpose. We rarely see the full picture, but God gradually reveals pieces of it over time. It is our job to assemble the puzzle and faithfully carry out our purpose. This guide will walk you through the process of prayerfully evaluating your God-given purpose and pursuing it!

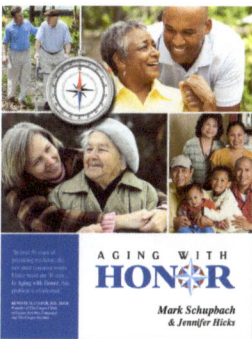

### Aging with Honor: A Practical Guide to Help You Honor Your Parents as They Age

Growing up is hard to do. That's why God gave kids parents — to teach, train, help, and guide them as they go from having a lot of limitations to having a lot of freedoms and into adulthood.

Growing old is even harder. That's why God gave parents kids — to encourage, support, help, and guide them as they go from having a lot of freedoms to having a lot of limitations.

This practical guide will cover a variety of issues in five individual segments: Financial Needs, Medical Needs, Logistical Needs, Relational Needs, and Spiritual Needs. It will provide you with the tools and resources that you will need in order to evaluate your situation and create a plan that works best for your family.

**To find out more about these and other resources or to place an order, visit our website:**

## www.LifeMarkMinistries.org

## Facebook.com/LifeMarkMinistries

## @LifeMarkMin

**Mark is available for speaking engagements and conferences. Please contact our office to discuss your event.**

www.ingramcontent.com/pod-product-compliance
Lightning Source LLC
Chambersburg PA
CBHW042124040426
42450CB00002B/67